The coloring book belongs to :

. . . .

Aa

Ant

Bb

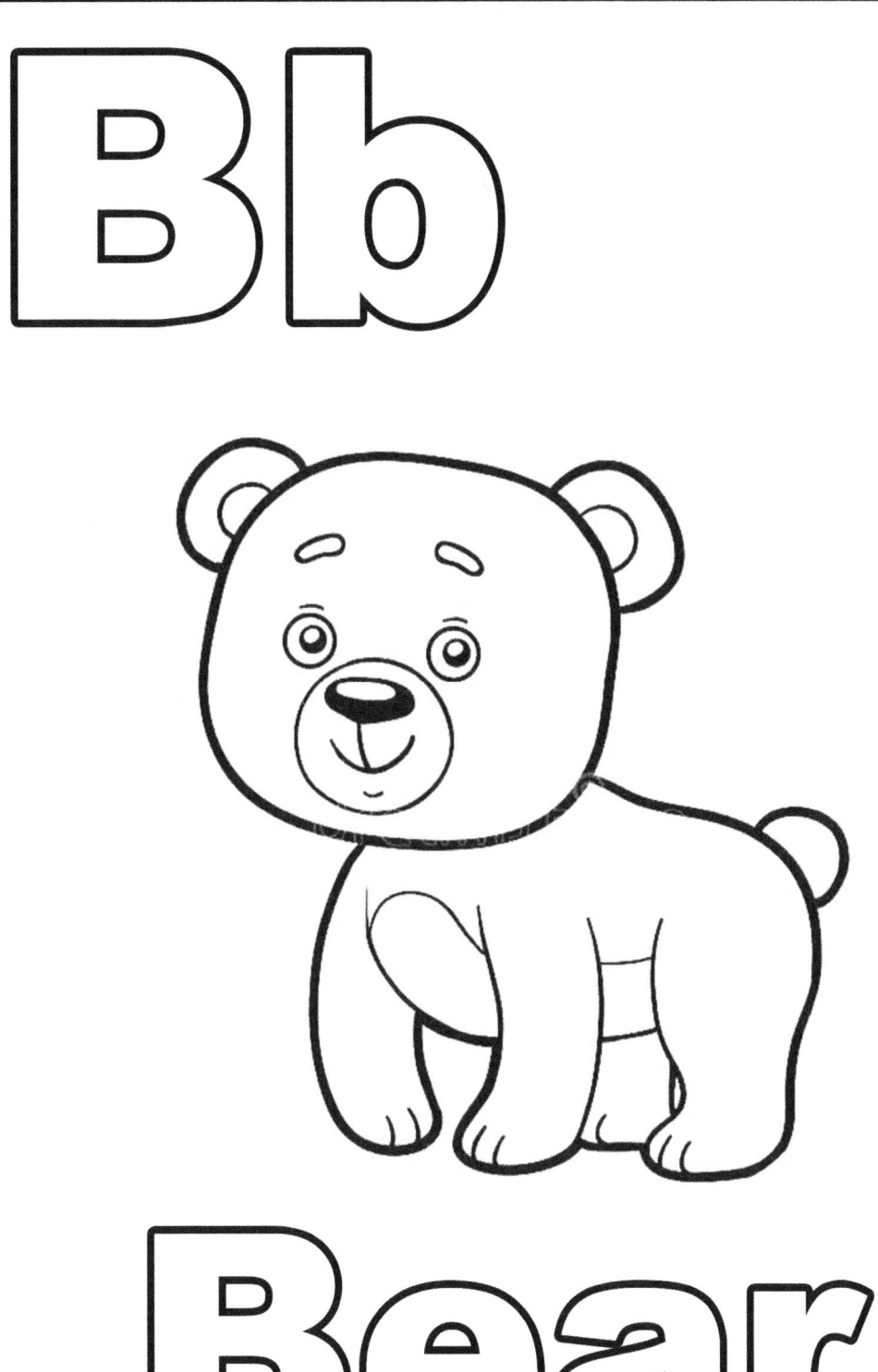

Bear

Cc

Cow

Dd

Deer

Ee

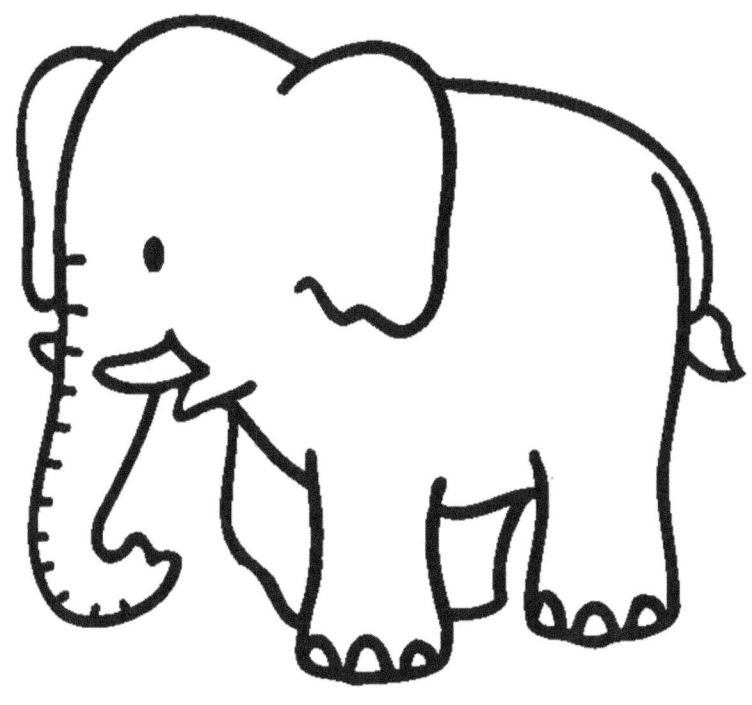

Elephant

Ff

Fox

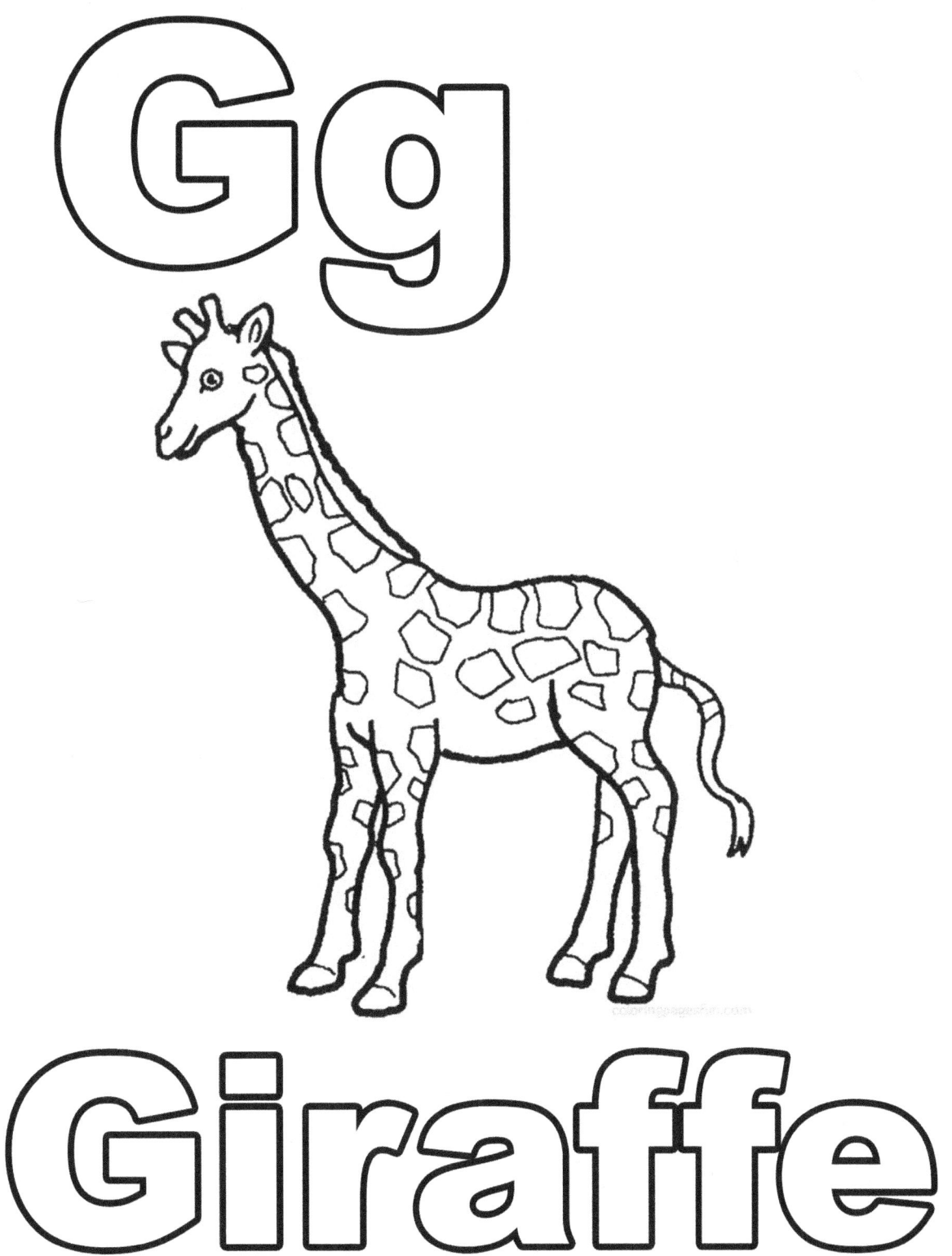

Hh

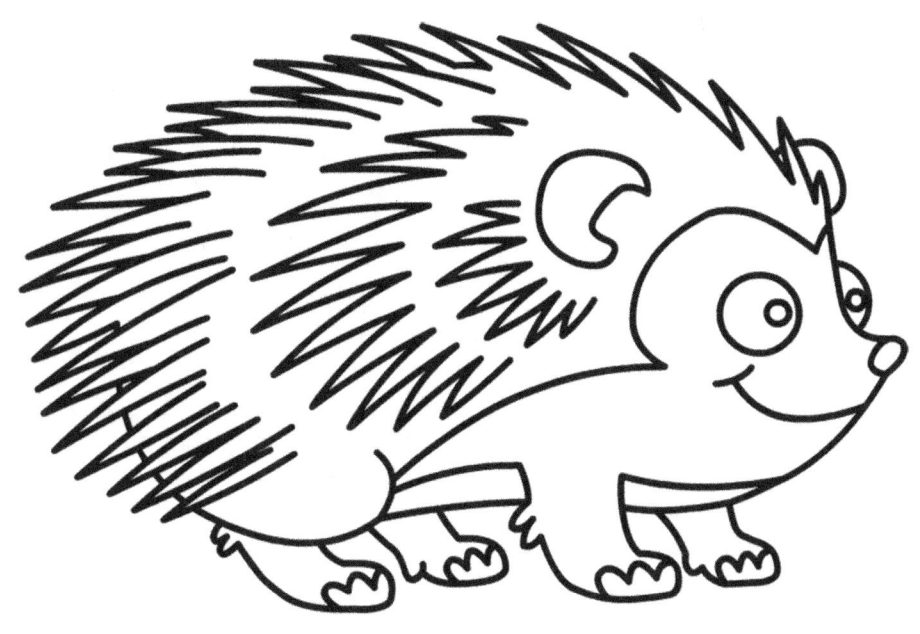

Hedgehog

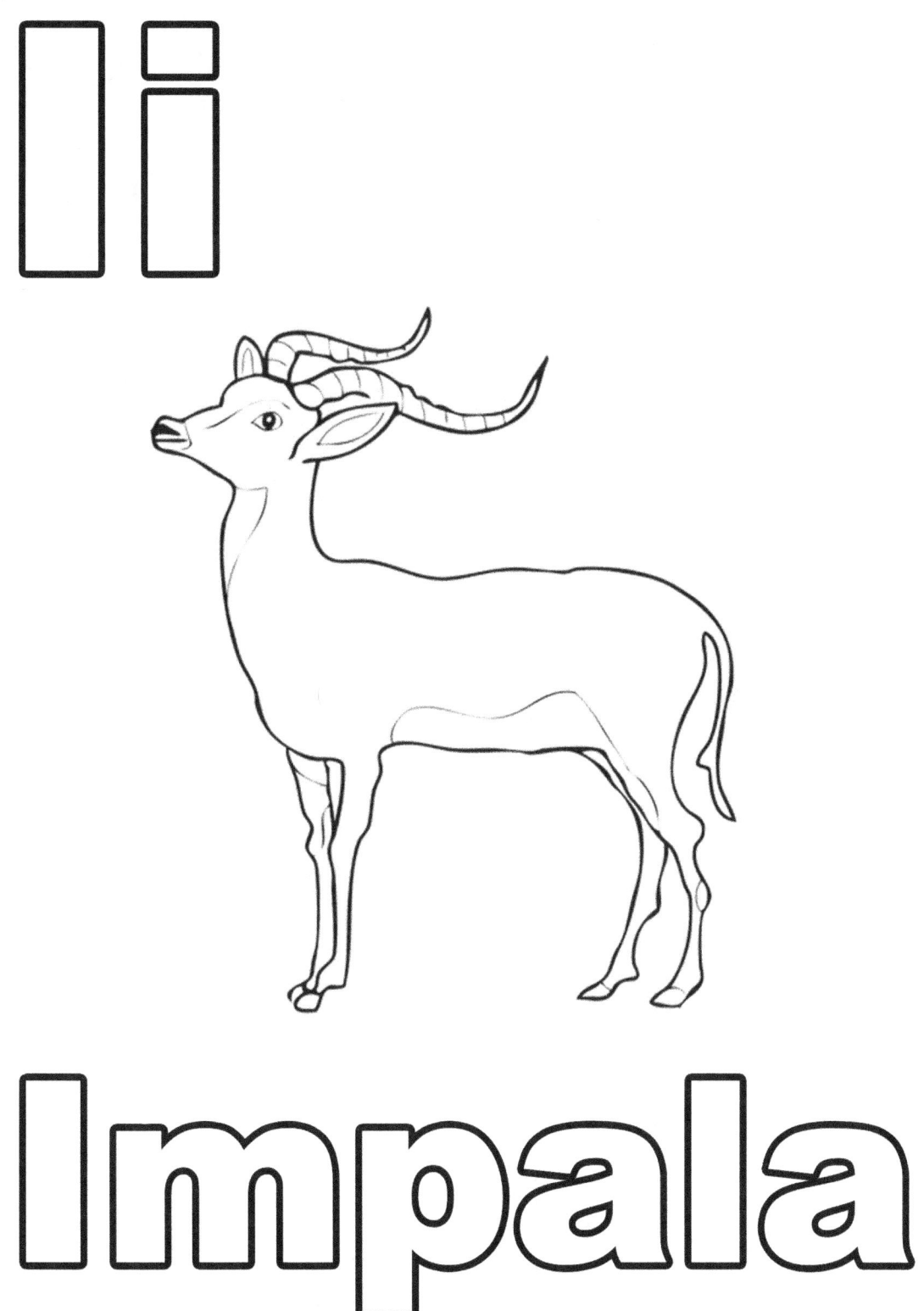

Ii

Impala

Jj

Jellyfish

Kk

Kangaroo

Ll

Lion

Mm

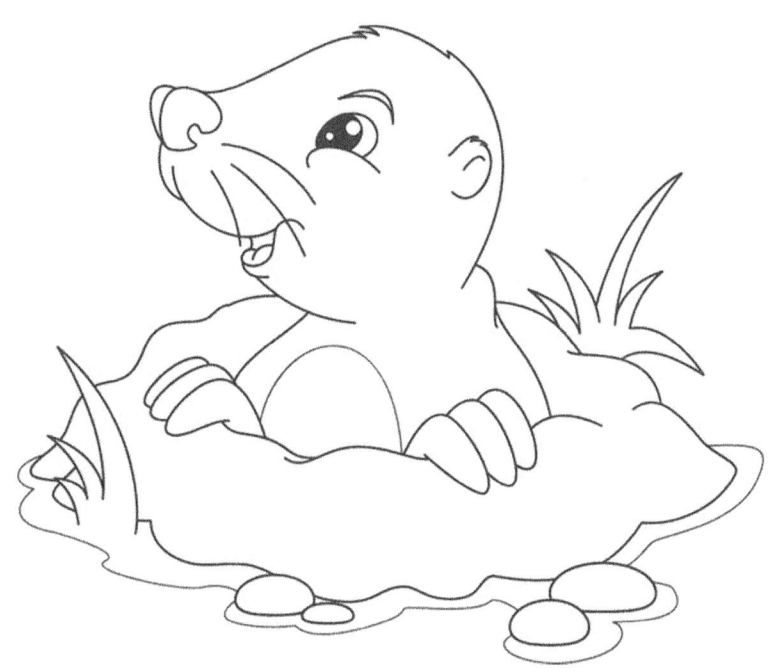

Mole

N n

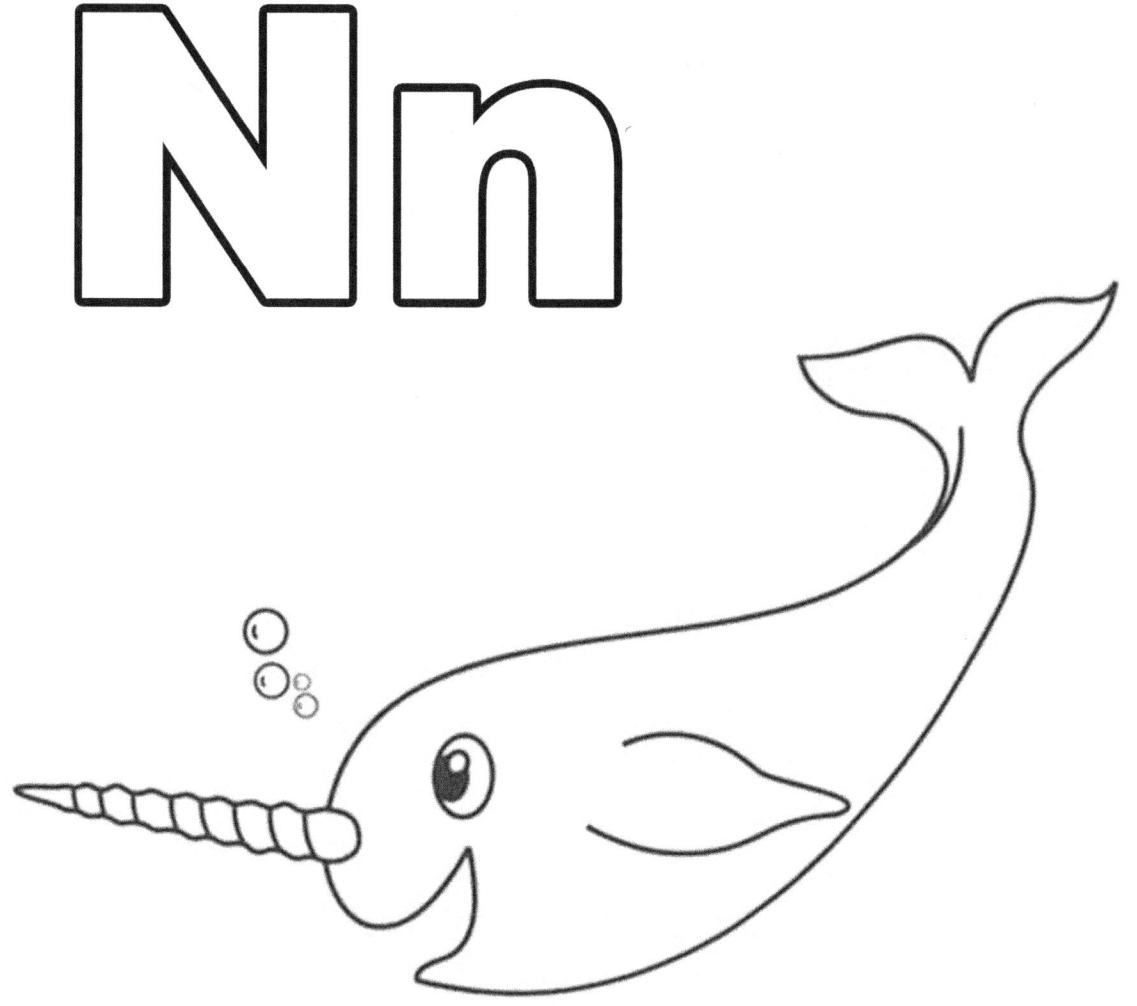

Narwahal

Oo

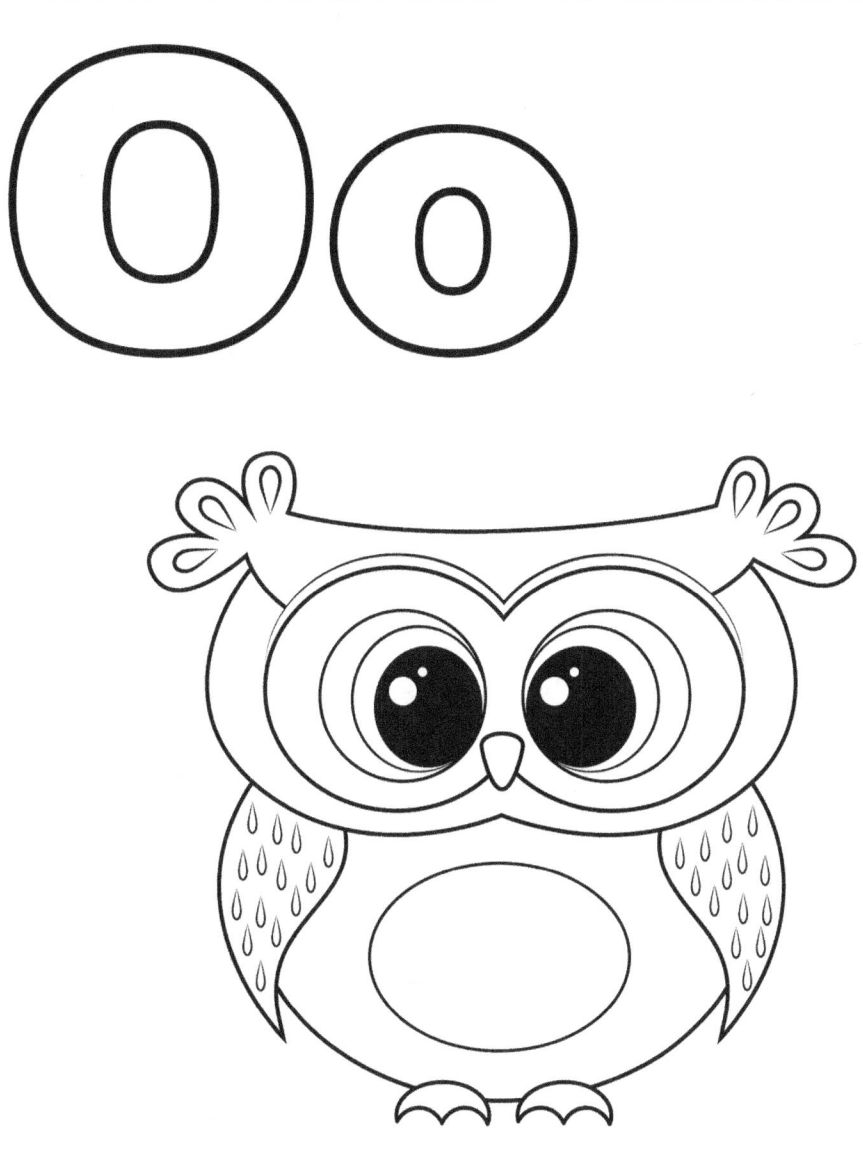

Owl

Pp

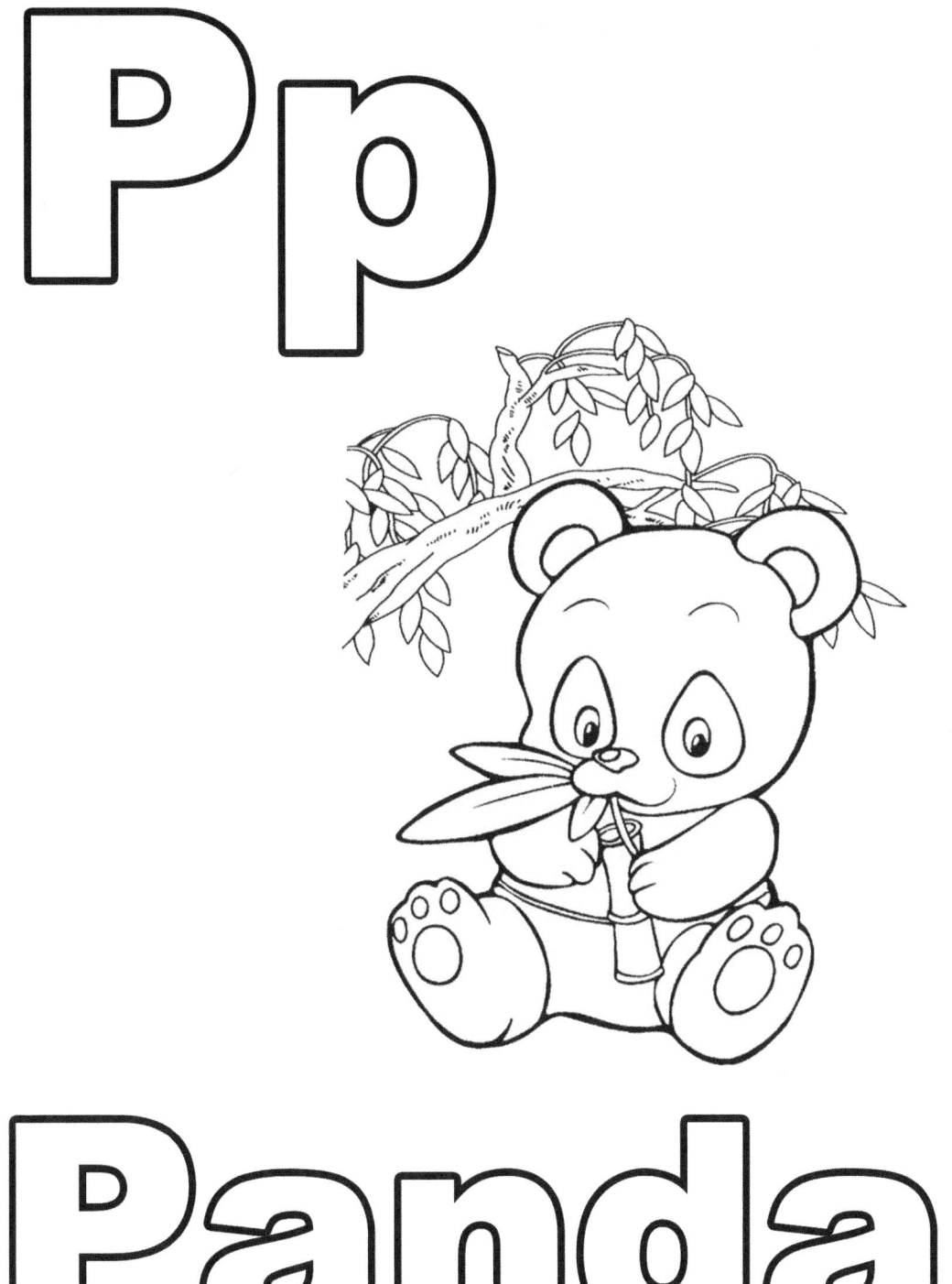

Panda

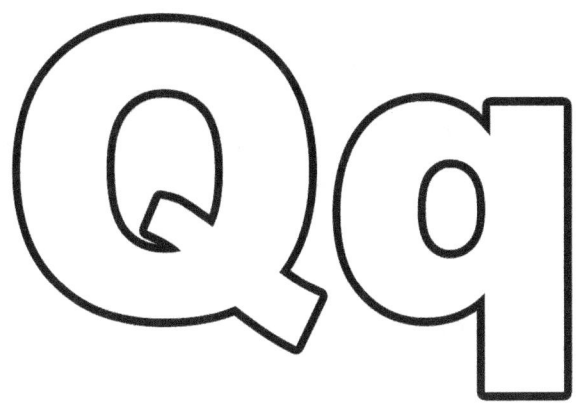

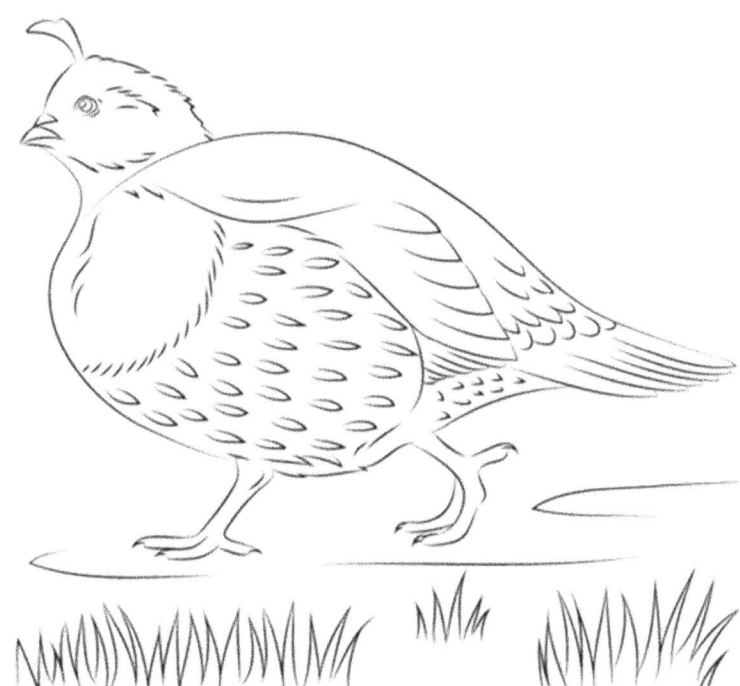

Quail

Rr

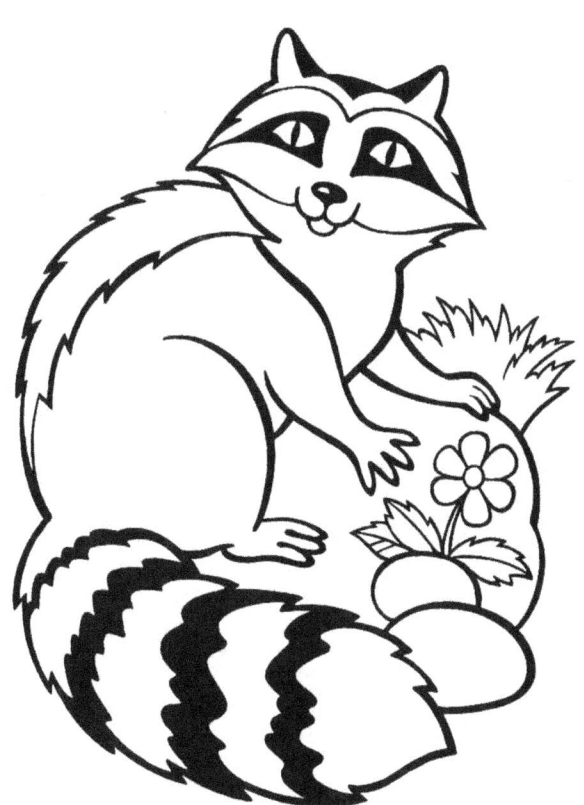

Raccoon

Ss

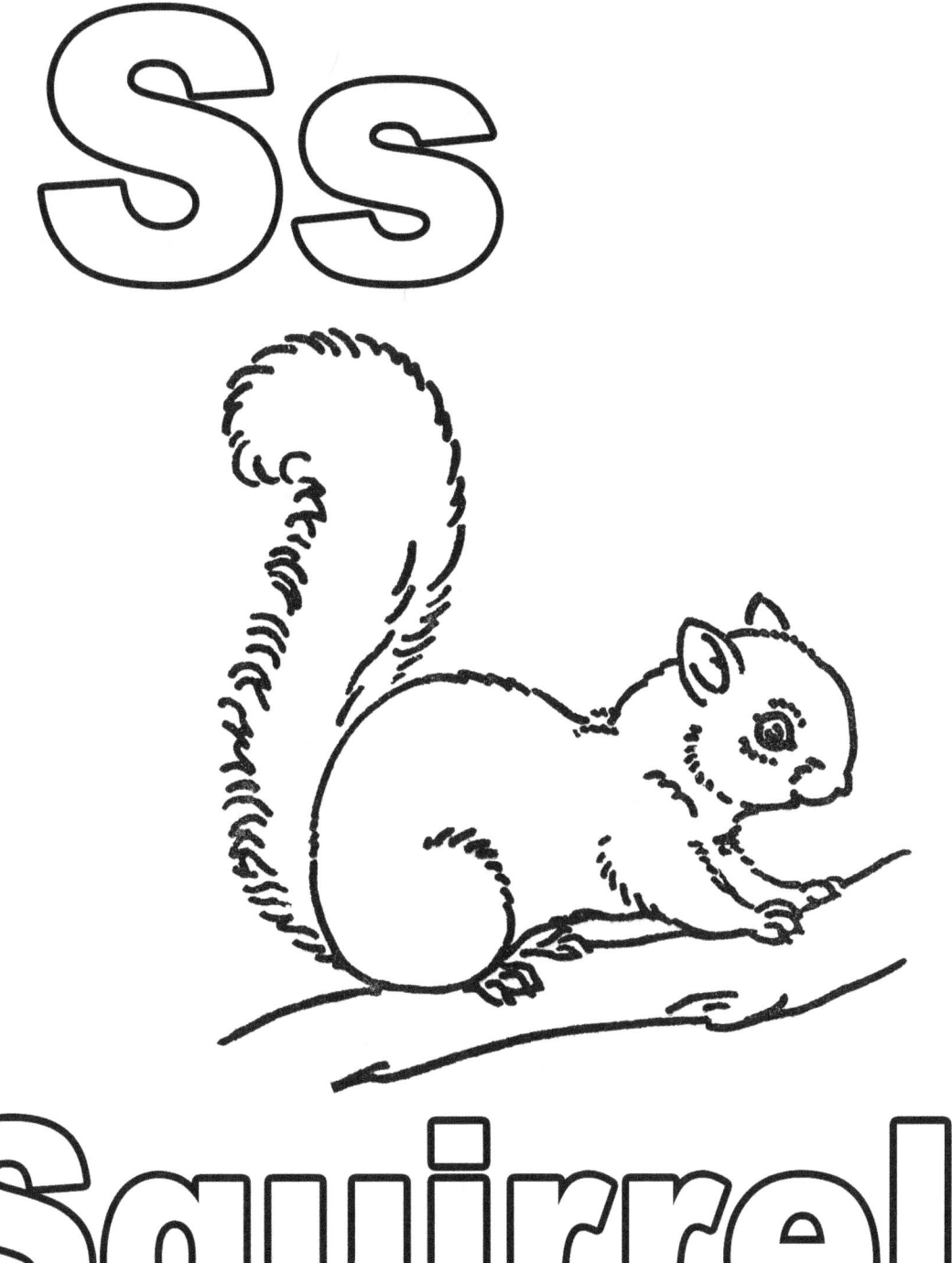

Squirrel

Tt

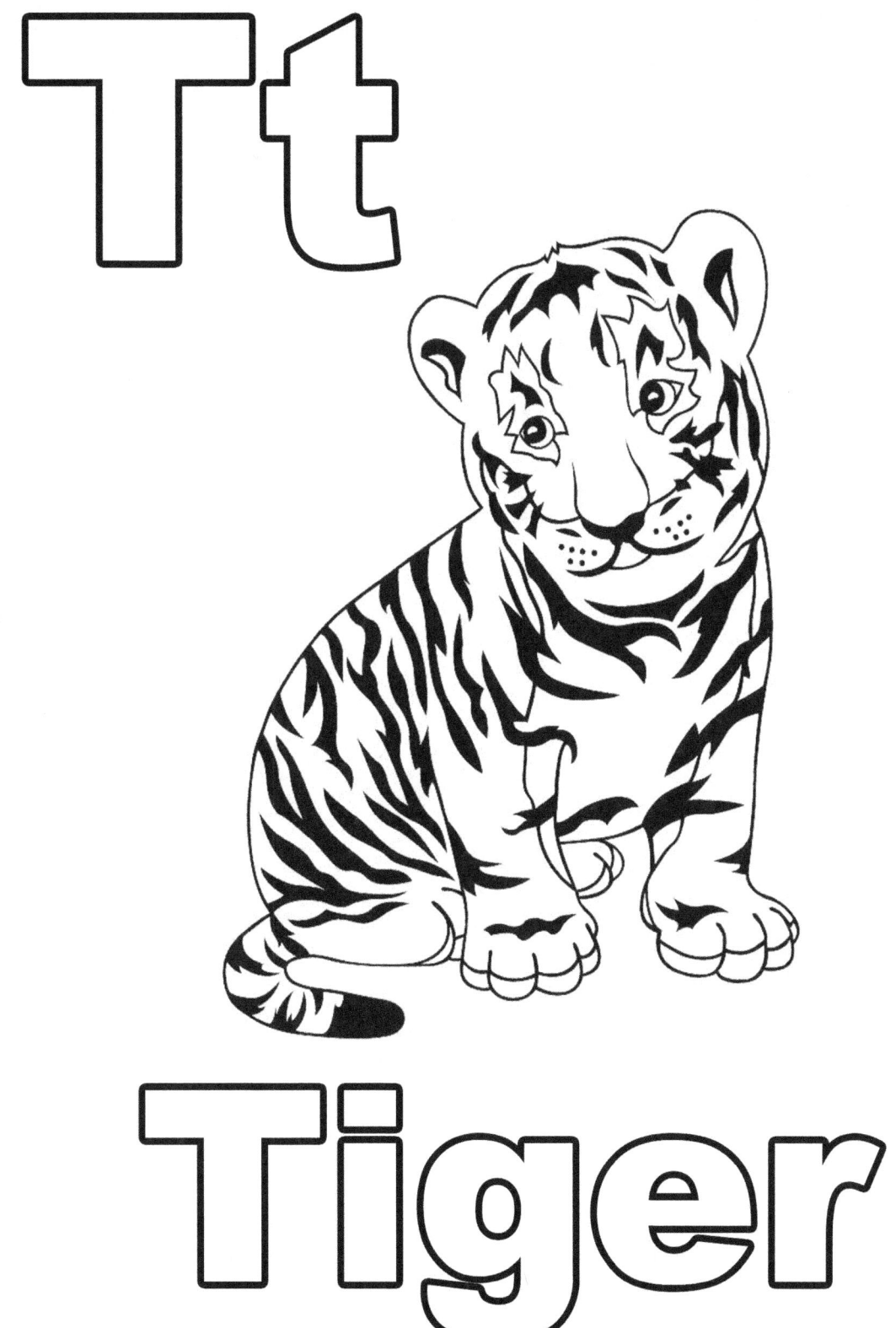

Tiger

Uu

Urchir

V v

Vulture

Ww

Wolf

Xx

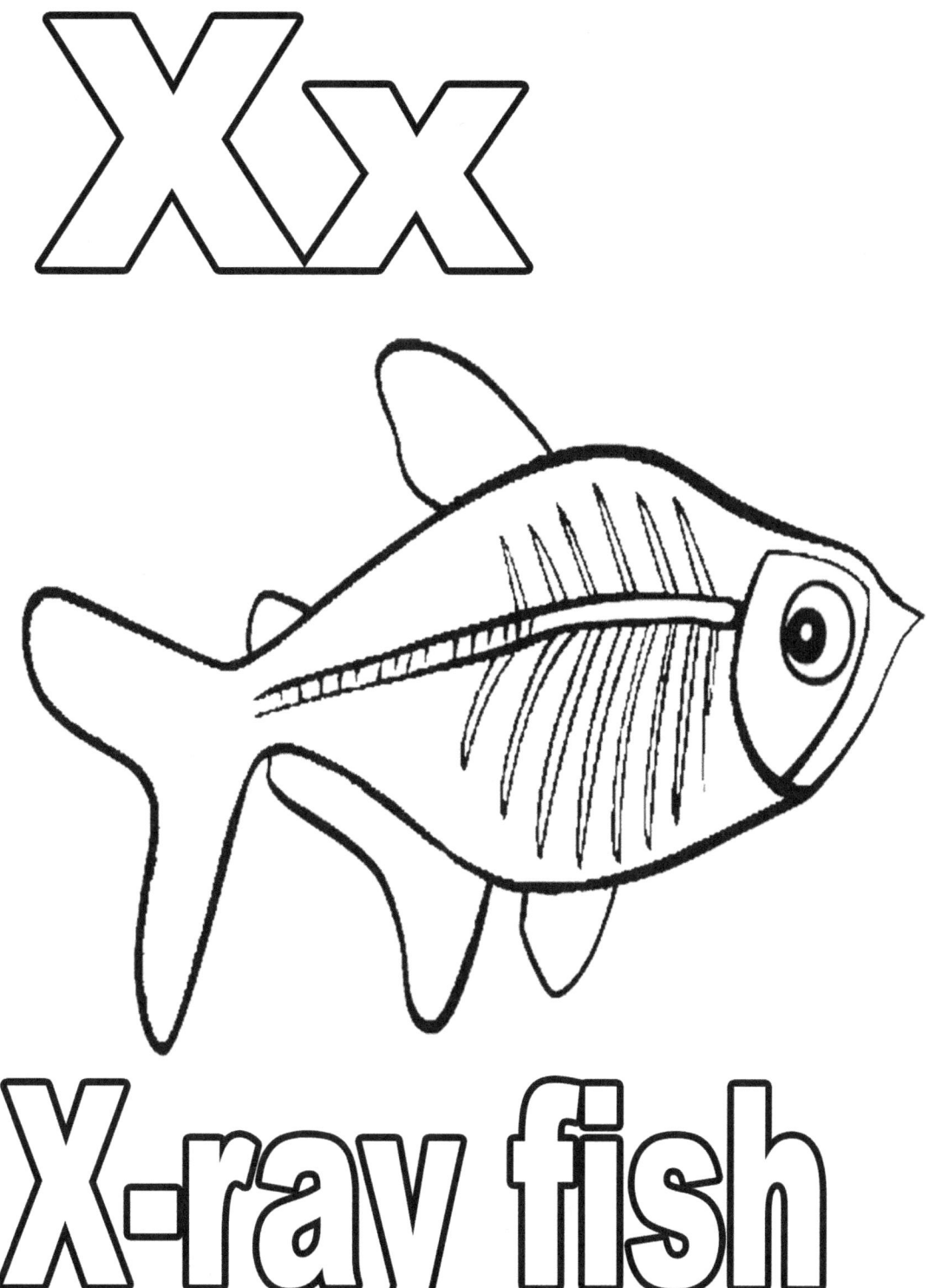

X-ray fish

Yy

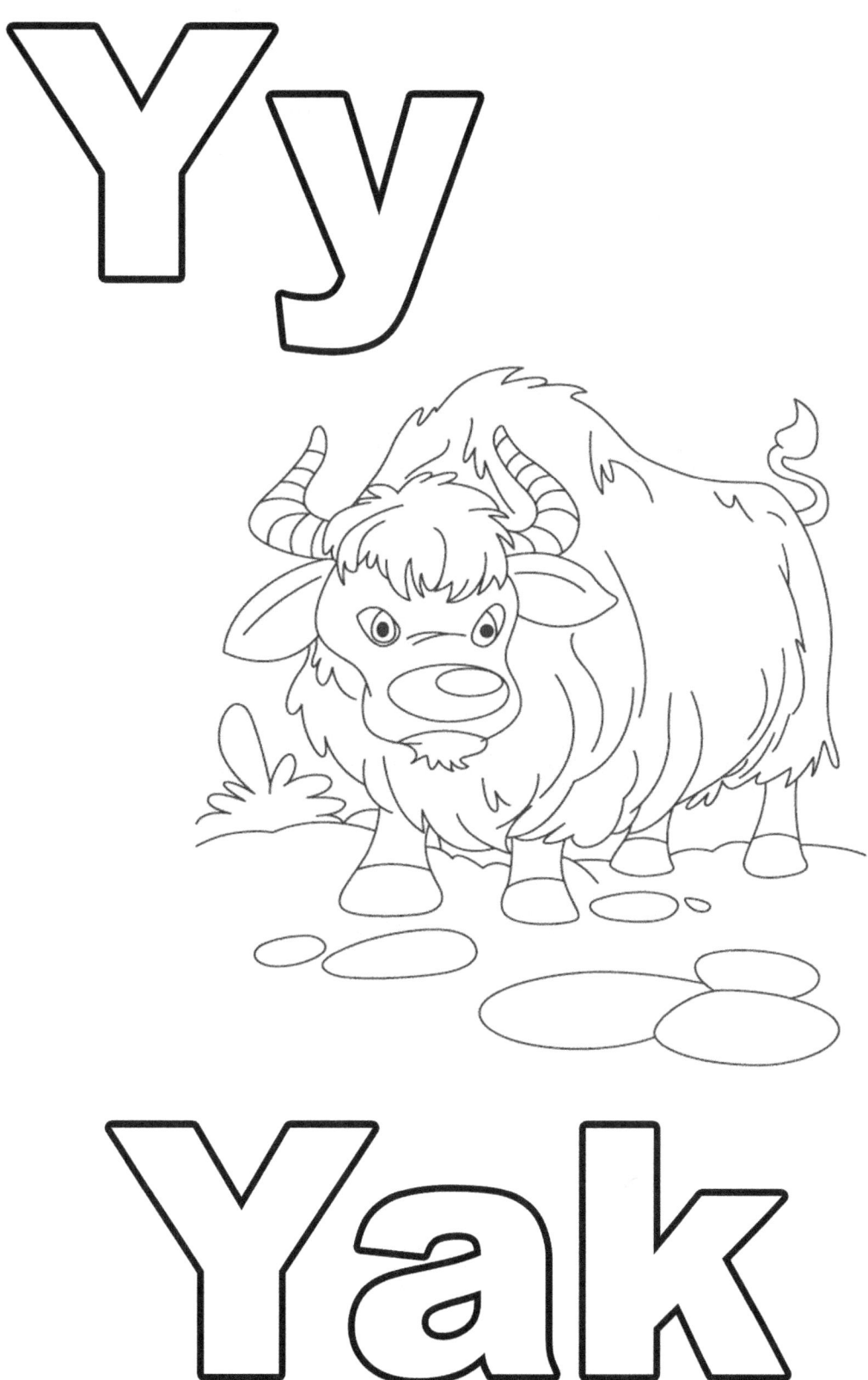

Yak

Zz

Zebra

www.ingramcontent.com/pod-product-compliance
Lightning Source LLC
Chambersburg PA
CBHW081004220526
45467CB00008B/2695